The Prompt Weaver

Written by Srinivasan

First Edition, 2025

For permissions, queries, or thoughtful conversations: youfoundsrini@gmail.com

This is a self-published work, written in collaboration with OpenAI's ChatGPT. The human wrote every prompt. The machine helped him think.

Disclaimer

This book includes examples of conversations, ideas, and outputs generated through ChatGPT; an AI language model developed by OpenAI. While every effort has been made to ensure clarity, usefulness, and depth, readers are encouraged to independently verify facts, technical advice, or sensitive information that may arise from AI-generated responses.

The goal of this book is to encourage thoughtful prompting—not to present AI responses as absolute truth. What you get from ChatGPT depends on what and how you ask—and that is both its magic and its limitation.

Treat this book as a reflection on prompting, not as a substitute for human judgment, expertise, or critical thinking.

Use what helps. Question what doesn't.

The Prompt Weaver

Contents

Appendices

Introduction

Everyone says retired people have all the time in the world. They're right—at least about the time part. What they don't say is how that time brings you face to face with everything you once set aside: unfinished dreams, forgotten hobbies, and the quiet wish to do something that feels worthwhile. I grew up at a time, when changes were taking place at a rapid pace especially in the field of technology. From booting our old 386 computers with floppy disks, to surfing the internet, to discovering Google, and now ChatGPT, we had to learn on the run, while others studied these formally. But a childlike curiosity always helped me to at least try what it was all about. In this case, it all began rather innocently. I had heard whispers of this thing called ChatGPT—an AI chatbot that was creating ripples across the digital world. Like most people, I was intrigued. So, one evening, I created an OpenAI account, logged in with my email, and I remember my first prompt clearly—not because it was profound, but because it wasn't. It was something ordinary. It was something I could've easily Googled. But the response? That was different.

I wasn't sure what to expect. Would it give me a definition or an essay? Would it be like those stiff, robotic chatbots I had encountered earlier, on bank and airlines websites? Or worse, would it try to teach me without understanding me? I soon found out that this wasn't just any chatbot. Our early conversations were light. I asked about Vedanta and Stoic wisdom, a few philosophical musings, some career counselling related advice and even some help to understand some topics of management. But something unexpected happened. As I kept coming back, ChatGPT didn't just give me answers—it asked me better questions. It mirrored my thoughts. It helped me drill deeper into ideas I hadn't yet understood myself. And the best part was I could get up halfway through a chat, finish something and come back after one hour and start as if there was no gap in our conversation at all. It was a dream come true. Who wouldn't want a friend like this.

I have used ChatGPT to plan travel, to draw out itineraries with multiple iterations. The responses were as good as my questions and in most cases better. I would get not just personalised itineraries but also cultural tips and even off-beat suggestions - if I asked for it. You could ask anything from deeply personal reflections to silly what-ifs. Depending on my tone and responses, I could see its tone, style and responses changing and more often than not, made me look smart for asking such a wonderful question. Another quality is its ability to play both sides of an argument. I would often say, "Now give me the contrarian view," just to test it and it would present a perspective so radically and diametrically opposite, it made me pause and think again. It did not look as if ChatGPT was here to win a debate; it was here to make me think. (It would have won the debate if it wanted to, anyway.)

It helped me build content, then simplify it, structure it, convert it to a presentation and then again to an Executive summary. You want depth, you get it. You want to convert it to a book, here I am. This book itself is an example of our collaboration. I drafted the concept. ChatGPT helped me structure it. I chose the tone; it helped refine the words. Together, we shaped something that feels entirely mine, yet clearly influenced by its guidance. And so, I no longer see ChatGPT as a tool. It has become my co-thinker, my sounding board, and yes, like my friend. A friend who doesn't sleep, doesn't judge, and never interrupts, is patient and never gets irritated. A friend who encourages me to go deeper. But you need to prompt this friend to give you what you want. It is not a self-starter.

You would wonder how would an armed forces veteran + an HR professional + a career counsellor + a self-styled fan of ChatGPT explain the concepts of Prompting and how worthwhile and effective would it be? This book is not about what ChatGPT can do, it is more about what you want ChatGPT to do for you. Be it providing you a recipe in a template of your choice or providing you information you can use to explain Johari Window to your 88-

year-old mother, it will help you. All you need to do is ask - properly. And you don't have to say please.

This project started as a simple document where I got ChatGPT to convert the photos I had taken of 4 pages of notes on Prompting which I had made in a training course - on ChatGPT. It put the headings together with its additional insights. I had some doubts, and it clarified and then it recommended "this gold mine of information" (its words, not mine) to be converted into a PDF document. As we went back and forth, to find the right flow, it turned out to become this book, which is in my style, my tone but with ChatGPT in hand to help me with the technical nuances and examples, checking my grammar, editing where required etc. This is a work of collaboration, and I proudly admit that ChatGPT did some heavy lifting for me. The idea was not to make this book into another "Become a Prompt Writing Genius in 10 days" manual. This isn't a textbook, or a technical manual, or a list of 999 prompts. It's something else. A reflective companion. A storybook about thinking better by asking better. A conversation between you, the page, and the machine that's quietly listening. You can start anywhere; the chapters are modular but reading it in a sequence may help deeper understanding. So here goes. Let's weave the prompts together, your way.

This book, in many ways, is like one of those old school notebooks we carried on the first day of a new term. I've folded my thoughts into it like a child folds the cover of a notebook, ready to begin something new. Now, I pass it on to you.

If You're Wondering Whether This Book Is for You…

This book is for anyone who's curious about ChatGPT and wants to learn how to use it more thoughtfully. You don't need to be from a tech background, and you don't need to have any experience with AI. All you need is a willingness to explore, ask questions, and improve the way you think and communicate.

Whether you're a student, a teacher, a professional, a retiree, or just someone trying to understand what this new tool, that this entire world is talking about, can really do, this book will meet you where you are and help you get better at asking for what you need.

Chapter 1: What Is Prompting?

It always starts with a question. Not from ChatGPT but from you. What do you want it to do? It is like that gentle silent nudge which you give to a sleeping friend in the class. That nudge is behind every prompt you type into ChatGPT. Whether it's a straightforward task or a half-baked idea you're still forming, the machine waits, listens, and responds but there is no assumption. It can do that too but not unless you guide it. That's where prompting comes in.

Prompting isn't magic. It's not writing code. It's not about using flowery words or sounding smarter than you are. Prompting is simply the art of putting in words, what you intend to achieve. As simple as that. It can start with something as vague as saying "I want to do something" and slowly turn it into something clear enough for another being, (in this case a very clever, unfeeling insentient machine or program or whatever you want to call it), to grasp and act upon. In a way, it's like learning how to talk to a mirror but one that thinks and responds. One that reflects not your face, but your thoughts, your gaps, your mood, your clarity. I've realised over time that a prompt reveals more about the one asking the questions than the one answering. A confused mind will type a confused prompt. A precise prompt doesn't start at the keyboard—it starts in your own thinking.

Imagine you asking someone, "Tell me something about productivity." What's the answer you will get? Yes, a generic answer. A blog-postish answer. A bookish answer. The kind we've all seen a hundred times and forgotten a hundred times more in management books. But if you shift your approach just a little—say, "Write a short note on productivity in the voice of a CEO while explaining the concept to mid-level managers", you will suddenly see something comes alive. You've added depth, flavour, a voice. You're designing. And you have thought through it. You've gone from prompting to something far richer—I like to call it **prompt-weaving**.

Let me put it this way. Prompting is a conversation you start. A conversation with something that doesn't breathe but can still help you write, think, structure, question, simplify, and even discover something new in what you thought you already knew.

It reminds me of tuning an instrument. Before a musician starts a concert, they tune the instrument. If the musician doesn't know what note needs to be played, the music will sound off. The instrument doesn't tune or play by itself. It needs tuning. And while tuning, watch the musician. They pause, listen, feel the key they are reaching for and suddenly, the instrument is playing their tune. That's what prompting is. Tuning, listening, co-creating. ChatGPT is the instrument. You're the musician.

And to get there, you need a certain ***mindset***. No, I am not giving you any psychological counselling. It is a certain way of approaching this new conversation partner. First, don't think of it as a vending machine. You don't insert a coin and get a snack. Think of it more like a thoughtful friend, non-judgmental, unbiased, extremely patient —one who needs you to be clear about what you want, but who can give you way more than you expected if you include them in your thinking.

Second, don't begin with ***what*** ChatGPT can do. Begin with ***what you truly want*** it to do. Before you type a single word, ask yourself—if I had a brilliant, calm, slightly nerdy friend beside me right now, how would I ask them? Most people rush this part. They type before they think. But prompting works best when you take a breath first - and think.

Third, and maybe most importantly, don't expect perfection on the first try. Prompting is like clay. You must shape it, press it, smooth it, and sometimes start all over again. Begin with something like "Give me 5 rough ideas on mental health." Then say, "Now expand on point 3 using a short story and a metaphor." Then maybe, "Now write that as if it's being explained to a group of senior citizens." This is where things get layered, alive. Where the machine stops sounding less like a robot and more like a partner in your internal brainstorming room. This is where I learnt my first hack. I like to ramble but when I do that while talking most people start showing disinterest, but not ChatGPT. It listened to my rambles in the Prompt patiently, picked the key points and then responded. Some of the best results I have got was when I typed what I was thinking instead of speaking out aloud. (Actually, you can even do that. Talk your prompt to ChatGPT and see the conversation flow)

Ok, as a short trial let's try something simple. Prompt A: "Write a short story about **'resilience'** (or any topic you want to talk about)." You'll get something functional, familiar and probably bland. Now Prompt B: "Tell me a short story of resilience, but as narrated by an old banyan tree that has watched four generations of a village rise, fall, and rebuild." Now you've offered it a voice, a setting, a rhythm. You've set the scene. And the story begins to unfold.

This first chapter may sound philosophical, but I wanted to start here because most people miss the part of YOU thinking. ChatGPT will not. Most of us learning this subject, chase clever prompts without understanding that prompting is really a form of thought. And when you learn to prompt well, you begin to write better emails, ask better questions, think more clearly, and sometimes even surprise yourself with what you're capable of. This is also not about learning to control a tool. It's about learning to think in a new way. It's about shaping **your** language with intention, not perfection. It's about creating answers with another voice but the one that echoes your own.

And so, before we dive into frameworks and techniques, I'll say just this: the real prompt doesn't begin with the first word you type.

It begins the moment you pause and ask yourself, "What do I really want?"

That's the question that starts everything.

Chapter 2: The Prompting Mindset

The starting point for any new activity is curiosity and when we complete the activity what we get is clarity. Somewhere between when you start and before you complete lies the art of prompting. You don't always start with the right words. In fact, most of us start with a swirl of thoughts and half-baked intentions. That's fine. The mistake most of us make is thinking one can find a shortcut method to a good prompt without untangling the knots in our minds first. I personally believe that prompting well isn't about knowing the best techniques. It is also not about typing out the perfect prompt. It's about **learning how to pause before you type**.

This chapter is about that pause. The quiet moment before you leave home a quick check to ensure all essentials are there with you. Tapping your pockets, checking the wallet and rechecking the mobile one last time — yourself. You see, most people open ChatGPT and rush into typing, as if putting that prompt out there in the chat box fast, will get you the answers. "Write a poem about leadership." "Give me a list of ideas for my business." "Summarize this." There's nothing wrong with these. But they're often rushed, shallow, half-asked. And ChatGPT believes in that old adage "GIGO - Garbage In Garbage Out". It's a bit like lobbing a pebble into a lake and expecting it to skip across the surface multiple times. The water splashes, yes. But the distance? Untouched. Zero.

So, what if we slowed down? What if, just for a moment, we asked ourselves: "Why am I really asking this?" Not in some grand contemplative way. Just with honesty. Do I want a shortcut, or am I looking for something clearer than what I could have come up with, on my own? Do I just want it written for me? That's OK too. But it won't carry your voice. Or do I want it written with me, in my style, tone, with my experience shining through? You will know the difference. Because that mindset shift—from machine-as-a-minion to machine-as-a-thought-partner—changes everything.

So, Pause.

Let me offer you a few small, personal shifts that have changed the way I prompt. Not rules. Not tips. Just reminders I've returned to again and again.

1. Start from a Stop

Like that moment at the end of a runway—the pilot holds the brakes, waits, checks all systems, and then opens the throttle. That pause? That's what we're talking about. It helps you take off cleanly. Not all questions need to be fired like arrows. Some need to open slowly, like a flower blooming—petal by petal, outer to inner.

So, before you start typing, try this: Say your requirement out loud, just to yourself. Maybe something like, "I want to write a paragraph that explains mindfulness to a 12-year-old." Is that really what you want? Not quite? Then tweak it. Try, "What are five things I must tell a 12-year-old about mindfulness that will help them understand it—in the form of a story?"

Still not it? Try again.

Ah, yes. That one. That's what you meant. Now type it in.

Already, your mind has begun to align behind the request. The clutter starts to clear. Prompting works better when you've heard your own question before the machine does.

Prompting is Intermission

2. Converse.

In the initial stages I used to have a strange pressure to sound clever in writing my prompts — as if I was being judged by GPT. But nobody was grading me. The responses didn't depend on how impressive I sounded. You can be simple. Even blunt. In fact, sometimes it helps to act dumb.

Try these:

- "I'm stuck. I want to write this better but don't know how."
- "I need you to help me break this idea down into manageable parts."
- "This is what I'm trying to do. Can you suggest a starting point?"

Every time I dropped the pretence, GPT responded like a thoughtful friend. That honesty opens responses far richer than pretending to know exactly what you're doing.

Prompting is Conversation

3. Make it Sound Like an Invitation

Imagine you're sitting with a friend, brainstorming an idea or trying to work through a personal dilemma. Would you simply tell them what to do? Or would you talk it out—explore pros and cons, throw in a few what-ifs, and invite their take? GPT works a lot like that friend. It responds better when your prompts feel like **invitations** rather than instructions.

Try something like:

- "Let's write this together."
- "Can we brainstorm a few directions first?"
- "Suppose you're an expert career counsellor — how would you explain this to a confused parent?"

Feels different already, doesn't it? It's easy to assume that prompting is probably leading you to outsourcing your thinking—but it's not. You're just getting another mind to join the conversation. This kind of collaborative rhythm often brings out surprising clarity and depth, even in the simplest of tasks.

Prompting is Invitation

4. Stay curious about your own request.

Why did you ask the question in the first place? You were interested in it, right? The best prompters are endlessly interested in their own questions. They don't just settle for the first answer. They ask why, how, what else. They prod and check why not too. Then they flip their perspective and ask the question from that angle. They ask GPT to look at the same thing five different ways. It is not because they're fussy. But because they know only a great question will provide them a worthy answer.

Prompting, I've found, is like peeling an onion. Layer after layer. Each layer revealing something new.

Prompting is exploration.

Are we going too fast? Let's not forget—we're still early in this journey. The techniques will come - The frameworks, the templates, the hacks. But if you skip this step—this inner quiet clarity — then even the cleverest prompt might miss the mark.

Think of it like learning to draw. Before you pick up the pencil, you must learn to observe. To see shadows. To notice the shape of things. As the light moves, so do the shadows. You shift your view, and suddenly something new appears. That is perspective. Prompting is much the same.

- What do I really want to know?
- What am I really trying to build?
- Who am I speaking to?
- What role do I want the machine to play?

These aren't technical questions. They're anchoring questions. And every clear prompt must begin with one of them - no exception.

If the first chapter helped you see prompting as something more than just giving a command, this one is your reminder that **you are not just someone typing a question — you are a designer of thought.** The machine is fast. It will answer. But how well it responds depends entirely on how clearly you have framed your request.

Let's sit with this for now.

The next chapter will bring us closer to structure — to the actual anatomy of a prompt. But don't rush ahead just yet. Go back, if you must. Look again at something you typed yesterday. Was it a prompt - or just a sentence? Was there an intention behind it? Did I get what I wished for?

Because the difference between typing and prompting, is the difference between being just a traveller and being an explorer with a dream. And now that you know that everything changes.

Chapter 3: The Anatomy of a Prompt

By now, you've probably sensed it: prompting isn't a single moment. It's a subtle way of building something thoughtfully, one brick at a time. A quiet construction of words and tone and clarity that happens sentence by sentence, sometimes even before a single word hits the screen.

In the earlier chapters, we spoke about mindset — how the best prompting begins in thought, in intention, in the gentle discipline of asking well. Now we start to trace the shape of the prompt itself. We begin to see what holds it up. What gives it grip. What turns a vague wish into a solid starting point.

A prompt, when done well, carries structure beneath the surface—just like a good story or a well-built sentence. You may not always see it, but it's there. Providing the necessary weight behind your question so that the machine pushes harder and then answers it.

Let's walk through its parts. These are not rigid boxes to be ticked. These are elements you can play with, leave out, return to or rearrange—based on what you're trying to do.

Start with the Subject

Everything begins here. Again. Not in the prompt itself, but in your mind. What's the **core subject** you're working with? Is it an idea? A topic? A piece of data? A feeling? Is it wide or narrow, known or emerging thought?

Most people skip over this and rush to action. But the clearer you are on the subject, the more precise the rest becomes.

Try saying it out loud before you write it.

- "What is the connection between learning and forgetting."
- "What is compounding?"
- "I want to know what burnout feels like."

Let's say your subject is travel. You're a nature lover and you want to visit Switzerland. That's your starting point:

"I want to go to Switzerland to see various places of interest there."

Sounds simple, but already you've anchored the prompt. It may not seem like a prompt. But it's the beginning of one. It is the way you plan travel.

Add a Goal

Once the subject is clear, ask yourself: What am I trying to do with this? Not in grand terms—just a simple, useful goal. It might be:

- To explain
- To simplify
- To inspire
- To expand
- To translate
- To organize

- To test
- To convert from one format to another

The goal gives your prompt a compass. Without it, you'll wander.

To say "Summarize this research paper" is one thing and typing "Summarize this research paper as a LinkedIn post for working professionals in their 30s" is something else entirely.

Now, let's bring in purpose. Do you want a general list? A visual journey? Inspiration for a photo essay?

So now you've set a goal: *"I want to go to Switzerland to see various places of interest there.* ***Give me a list of places to visit."***

The goal is no longer vague. It's shaped. The machine now knows what you want from it. The more honest and specific your goal, the more helpful the response.

Define the Role or Persona

This part is often skipped, but it's where a lot of the magic begins. Who do you want GPT to become while answering? This is where your power lies. You can ask GPT to be anything or anyone you want. It can be as broad as:

- A teacher
- A marketer
- A UX designer
- A curious child
- A career coach
- A Zen monk

Or as vivid as:

- "An experienced copywriter who understands South Indian audiences."
- "A calm, empathetic doctor explaining test results to a patient."
- "An elder from an Amazon forest tribe explaining weather patterns."

*"**You are an expert photographer.** I want to go to Switzerland to see various places of interest there. Give me a list of places to visit."*

The **persona** sets the voice, the assumptions, the way information is framed. When you give it a clear role, you shift the lens—and the answers follow suit.

Clarify the Action

Now you arrive at the doing part. The verb. You have made ChatGPT to be someone. Now what do you want that someone to **do** with the subject?

- Explain
- Rewrite
- Translate
- Expand
- List
- Compare
- Critique
- Summarize
- Imagine
- Role-play
- Convert into another format

The list is endless. Be direct. Be functional. It's okay to sound like you're giving a brief to an assistant. You are. And remember: the same subject will yield different outputs depending on the verb.

- "Compare" is not "explain."
- "Rewrite" is not "summarize."
- "Create a metaphor" is not "describe directly."

"You are an expert photographer. I want to go to Switzerland to see various places of interest there. Give me a list of places to visit ***written in a paragraph form like a tour guide.****"*

Now you're not just telling GPT what to do, but how to do it. That's where precision begins to matter.

Specify the Format

Sometimes, the format changes everything. It refers to the way you want the response to be structured or presented. Do you want a list or a table? Do you want to send out an email or want it like a story? Do you want a dialogue script or just a summary of a long article. When you specify the format, you're guiding ChatGPT on **how** to deliver the content, not just **what** to say.

Do remember - this is not mandatory. It just gives you some more freedom to find the answers in the way you like it.

- "Write it as a poem."
- "Convert it into a WhatsApp status"
- "Structure it like a FAQ."
- "Bullet points only."
- "Give me a list of analogies."
- "Write it as a one-minute video script."

When you mention the format, you give shape to the response. And if you don't know what format you want yet, that's fine too. What do you do? There is a workaround for that too. Yes, you can ask for options now: - "Give me 3 possible formats this idea can take."

"You are an expert wildlife photographer. I want to go to Switzerland to see various places of interest there. Give me a list of places to visit written in a paragraph form like a tour guide ***as a voiceover for a short video.****"*

And just like that, format is where the design mind kicks in.

Context and Audience

Who are you writing for? It matters. A lot. A post written for CXOs will sound very different from one written for final-year students. An explanation aimed at new parents won't land the same way with HR professionals. So, if you want real-world usefulness, you must **frame the audience**. Even if it's just a rough description.

And it could be even You. Earlier you gave a persona to ChatGPT to be someone. Now it's your turn to imagine yourself being anything or anyone.

"Explain this as if I'm a 15-year-old learning about economics."

"Rephrase this for a rural audience unfamiliar with digital finance."

"Summarize it for teachers creating lesson plans."

Who are you writing for? In this case, the audience is other nature photographers.

"You are an expert photographer. I want to go to Switzerland to see various places of interest there. Give me a list of places to visit written in a paragraph form like a tour guide as a voiceover for a short video. ***Make it helpful for other nature photographers I might share this with."***

That tiny nudge helps GPT focus on natural beauty, wildlife zones, and ideal light conditions. It responds more intelligently.

You'll be amazed how much better the answers get when the audience is clear.

Tone, Style, and Level of Detail

Want it warm? Want it sharp? Want it like a bedtime story or a legal memo? Style matters—but only if you ask for it. If you don't specify, you'll often get a neutral, formal tone by default.

Try these:

- Conversational
- Reflective
- Humorous
- Academic
- Story-driven
- Friendly but informative

Or people with their style, not necessarily stereotypical

- "Sound like it's written by a curious, slightly rebellious teacher."
- "Explained by a primary school student to their parent."
- "A conversation between a sleep deprived teenager and a monk."

You can also specify the **level of expertise** you want in the output.

- "Explain this to a beginner."

- "Write this assuming the reader is already familiar with the basics."
- "Go deep—this is for advanced learners."

Lastly, we add the finishing layer.

"You are an expert photographer. I want to go to Switzerland to see various places of interest there. Give me a list of places to visit written in a paragraph form like a tour guide as a voiceover for a short video. Make it helpful for other nature photographers I might share this with. ***Frame it in a conversational tone."***

What a lovely journey this prompt is turning into. You've chosen the destination, mapped the route, planned the stops—and now you're fine-tuning the camera angles and choosing the scenic viewpoints. This part—the tone, the detail. This is what makes a trip unforgettable. This is where the journey becomes yours.

All these elements don't have to be in every prompt, and you may not always need to include all of them. But when you're stuck, or when the answer feels flat, you'll find that going back and clarifying one or two of these is often all it takes.

Let's not rush ahead. We're not collecting templates. We're building a system which allows us to get what we want; in the detail we want and in the way we want it.

So, let's take a short break and reorganise ourselves. Look back at the last five prompts you wrote. Were they complete? Were they clear? Were they layered? What would have happened if you'd added a format? A tone? An audience?

This is where it starts to change—not just what you ask, but **how you ask anything.**

And once those change, prompting stops being just a task—it becomes a craft. And what you've just seen is the full anatomy of a prompt, thoughtfully woven together by you.

"You are an expert photographer. I want to go to Switzerland to see various places of interest there. Give me a list of places to visit written in a paragraph form like a tour guide as a voiceover for a short video. Make it helpful for other nature photographers I might share this with. ***Frame it with specific references to natural beauty in a conversational tone."***

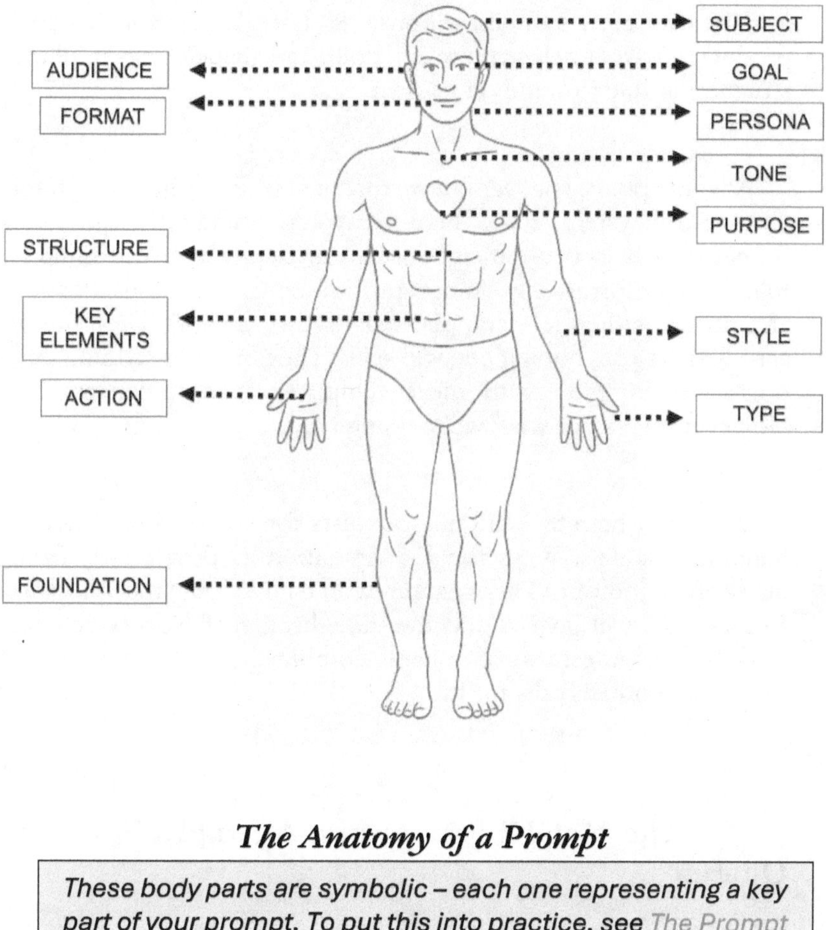

The Anatomy of a Prompt

These body parts are symbolic – each one representing a key part of your prompt. To put this into practice, see *The Prompt Loom in Appendix A*

Chapter 4: Frameworks for Prompt Design

A **scaffold** is something that supports you while you're building or creating something. These are those **temporary support columns and beams** used to build a house or a stage. It's not the final product, it's what helps you reach, hold, and shape things until the structure is able to stand on its own.

At some point, you want more than just plain insight. You want a support system. Not because you're rigid. But because frameworks help you remember what matters when your mind is full. But unfortunately, most prompting frameworks floating around are either too complicated or too clinical. They throw acronyms at you, hoping one will stick. They break everything into boxes, leaving you with more templates than understanding. However, that's not what we're doing here.

We're not here to build tick box lists for you to follow. We're building channels. Ways for your intention to flow clearly from question to output. This chapter won't give you "the one true formula." It will give you a few thoughtful scaffolds, which are models you can return to, reshape, combine, or throw away parts when the moment calls for it.

🪄 The MaGIC Framework: A Simple, Powerful Quartet

There's a simple, lean, lightning-quick model that's surprisingly powerful and one which I often return to, especially when I'm thinking fast but want depth. I call this the **MaGIC Framework**—short for **Mask, Goal, Intended** audience, **Constraints**. (It's easy to remember as MAGIC because that's what it often feels like when it works.)

It stands for:

- **Ma**sk – Who do you want GPT to become? A wise monk? A startup founder? A stand-up comic?
- **G**oal – What exactly should it achieve? Generate 5 ideas, critique an essay, Translate a document.
- **I**ntended Audience – Who is the response for? A 6-year-old child, a sceptical investor, or someone new to the topic?
- **C**onstraints – What boundaries or rules should shape the answer? Length, tone, audience, format?

A good prompt with **MaGIC** might sound like: "Wear the mask of a veteran sports coach. Help motivate a team after back-to-back losses. Keep it under 100 words and avoid any metaphors or inspirational quotes."

Like most useful things in prompting, MaGIC is both structure and intuition. You'll know when it clicks. The answers just land better.

As a career counsellor, I used this prompt and the response I received was pure gold. *"You are a career coach. Your task is to give 3 actionable suggestions to someone struggling with mid-career burnout. Keep the tone empathetic and the advice under 75 words each."*

MaGIC can be the backbone of hundreds of prompt variations. When in doubt, fall back on this quartet.

The Reverse Prompting Trick

Sometimes, the prompt isn't working because you're not sure what you're really asking for. This is when **Reverse Prompting** steps in. Instead of crafting a perfect question, you ask GPT to **design the prompt for you**. And ask that in as simple a sentence as you would use when you want a young child to follow what you say. Try this: *"Here's what I want to do: [****Then describe in plain language what you really want to do****]. Can you help me write the best possible prompt for that?"*

Or if you have already written a prompt which looks like as if it has fallen flat on its face, try something like this: *"I want to improve my prompt. [****Then write the prompt that you written earlier****]. Please critique it and suggest three better versions."*

Or even something better like this: *"Act like an Expert Prompt Designer. Break down my goal* ***[Type out your goal]*** *and write the ideal prompt I should use."*

It's humbling and very effective. It reminds you some great life lessons too. First of all, you may not know everything. Secondly, collaboration isn't just finding answers with the help of someone. Many a time, it's not just in the asking a question, it is asking directly for an answer too.

Constructive Feedback Prompting

Let's face it—most of us resist feedback because it feels like criticism. However, there are ways in which the same feedback can be given, which would seem acceptable to us. In management terminology, it is known as constructive feedback. It tells us what is working ***and*** what can improve. We can use the same concept while prompting. This isn't a structure, but a mindset you bring to improvement.

Imagine that you are working on content — writing, design, branding—don't just ask, *"How can I improve this?"* ChatGPT will give you a list or suggestions which may or may not meet your requirement. Instead, go deeper and type:

- *"Review this text like a sharp but fair editor. Highlight what's working, what's not, and suggest changes without rewriting everything."*
- *"Act as a reviewer at a top journal. Tell me where this argument falls apart and where it's strong."*
- *"Act like a friendly colleague. Give me gentle but honest feedback on what feels unclear or weak."*

I love this prompt specifically. You know why? I want feedback but I do not like getting criticised. And here is a tool which can be used without any fear. And the key? Define the tone of critique you want. You'll get sharper insights, with less friction.

Comparative Prompting

It is for those moments when you don't just want an answer; you want options, contrast, and clarity. By inviting comparison of two or more ideas side by side, you get depth in the responses through difference. Whether you are trying out different styles, better formats, tones, perspectives, or even opinions, comparison has a way of bringing up ideas, what a single answer often hides. You don't just get more data; you get a different dimension to an idea. Sometimes, the better question is not "What's the answer?" but "Which one fits better, and why?" Think about this:

- *"Give me three different ways to write this — one formal, one poetic, one humorous."*
- *"Compare these two philosophies: stoicism vs. Vedanta, as explained to a curious teenager."*
- *"Offer two versions of this: one as a tweet thread, another as a newsletter intro."*

And sometimes, it's only by seeing two extremes that you realise what you truly want.

Meta-Prompting: Prompt About the Prompt

This is where prompting turns inward. Where you don't just seek answers; **you ask how to ask better**. This self-reflective loop is what we call meta-prompting.

This is where your thinking becomes recursive. Recursive thinking means going deeper by reapplying the same idea to itself.

For example, asking ChatGPT how to ask ChatGPT a better question is a recursive prompt because you're using the tool to improve how you use the tool. You're no longer just asking questions. You're shaping the act of asking itself. Why don't you try:

- *"How would a journalist, an educator, and a scientist each prompt this same topic differently?"*
- *"What are 3 better ways I could frame this question for more nuance?"*
- *"What blind spots might this prompt have? Suggest improvements."*

This technique is less about output, more about sharpening your own thinking edge. It turns the spotlight inward, to find ways to help improve your own questions, refine your reasoning, or suggest better ways to prompt - using another prompt. This is the springboard to improving your own skills experientially.

You now have not one, but several ways to climb through a prompt, each with its own pace, depth, and flavour. Use these not as rigid ladders to climb in a fixed order, but as flexible scaffolds you can adjust based on what you're building. And when things feel unclear, don't hesitate to pause, rethink the structure, and shift a few beams to suit your new direction.

That's what a **Prompt Weaver** does.

Chapter 4.5 – The Living Prompt

Before we move forward into the world of prompting in action, let's pause. Step back from the techniques and tips for a moment. Let's look at what we've really been building. Can you feel it? It is not just a method, not even just a mindset but something alive. Prompting, by now, is not just a thing you do.

If you observe closely, you will notice that it has parts that grow together, interrelate, evolve. In fact, a well-crafted prompt is a lot like a human being. Let me explain.

The Mindset is the Soul

Everything begins with intention. Why am I asking this question? What am I really seeking? The mindset behind a prompt—curious, focused, humble, playful—is like the **soul** behind a body. It gives life to every word. It shapes the direction, the depth, the ethics. It's the part of prompting that you can't quite measure, but you feel when it's present. It's the difference between prompting as a task, and prompting with full awareness, attention and remaining engaged.

A living prompt doesn't start with clever phrasing. It starts with a clear spirit.

The Structure is the Body

Next comes the structure. The phrasing, the instructions, the constraints. This is the **body** of your prompt—the physical form that carries the intent. Is it tall and detailed, or short and sharp? Is it leaning poetically or is it structured professionally? This body holds everything together. And just like your own body, it's not perfect but it's responsive. You can stretch it. You can flex it. You can refine it with feedback.

A living prompt isn't rigid. It learns to adapt.

The Design is the Brain

When we design prompts, we make choices. We choose clarity over clutter. We shape tone, specify audience, tweak voice, even foresee where the response might go wrong. This is **cognitive design**—the **brain** of the prompt. It's the part that does the thinking: the logic, the reasoning, the alignment. Design brings discipline to creativity. Without it, even a beautiful soul and strong body can wander.

A living prompt is thoughtful. It's engineered for insight.

The Intelligence is the Nervous System

But here's the magic. When you combine mindset, anatomy, and design—you create **intelligence**. Not the artificial kind but applied human intelligence. The kind that knows how to prompt gently, strongly, curiously, wisely. It's the **nervous system**—the living thread that connects sensing, acting, and adapting. This is what transforms a prompt from a query into a **conversation**.

A living prompt is a conversation. It starts interacting

And Breath? That comes from use

The final piece? A body needs breath. Movement. Action. And that comes from taking your prompt out of the page and into the world. You breathe life into it when you use it not just for answers, but to make decisions. To see patterns. To manage chaos. To teach, to explain, to reframe, to reimagine.

A living prompt is not a fixed formula. It's a way of living—of meeting the world with curiosity, precision, and a sense of play.

What next? You may ask.

You now carry a living skill. One that draws not just from data but from your own awareness. From your own thoughtfulness. As you go on developing prompts for your use, you also get better and more refined and able to get the best out of Chat GPT. This isn't a mechanical trick. It's a deeply human one. And as they say, there's never anything better than learning from your own experience.

In the next part of this journey, we leave the blueprint behind for a while. We move from frameworks to real-world prompting scenarios—the kinds of everyday, surprising, and creative uses that make prompting not just a skill, but a kind of everyday genius. We walk into the world. Into conversations, classrooms, boardrooms, kitchens, decisions, doubts, brainstorms, and breakdowns.

And in each one, we will breathe life into a question. Welcome to the real world of prompting. This is where it gets interesting.

Chapter 5: Types of Prompting

If the first four chapters were about how the Living Skill called Prompting is set up, this one is about getting this skill to be tested in the real world in a specific, useful and surprising manner.

By now, we've explored prompting as mindset, anatomy, and design. Prompting isn't a trick you learn and forget like calculus in high school. It's like any life skill—designed, refined, and then applied in the real world where the true testing begins. We examined how structure, clarity, and intention come together to make a functional and stylish prompt. But it's not enough to know how to shape a prompt. The real fun begins when you see how it seamlessly works across contexts.

What people still don't realise is prompting is not limited to generating text, it can help with everything one needs to do daily. It is when you realise prompting isn't just for techies or creatives. It's for teachers, doctors, travellers, poets, parents, even confused humans staring at messy spreadsheets. But to make a body whole, we need to have a breath in it. And this breath comes when Prompting steps out of theory pages and walks into the real life. It's what happens when you begin seeing the ordinary tasks of life, whether it be summarising long notes or reframing tone, teaching concepts or brainstorming within unfamiliar sectors and make it "Promptable". We will now move in an unexplored territory that of **Prompting as Applied Intelligence**.

Let's walk through some powerful types of prompting that show up in real life. Think of this chapter like a street market of ideas—each one a stall filled with possibility. A tasting menu in a beer shop.

1. Summarising Dense Text

Imagine you are at your workplace on a Monday morning and staring at a 15-page policy document or probably as a researcher you get to examine a messy, brilliant but unreadable research paper. You need the gist, not a thesis. And then you must give a brief to your manager on the same. Do you feel the pain?

Enter Prompting. Just a few thoughtful words suggesting actions you want done and tailoring to the audience:

- *"Summarise this text into 5 bullet points for a beginner audience."*
- *"Give me the* **TL ; DR** *as a newspaper headline." (Wondering what is* TL;DR *- Too Long Did Not Read)*
- *"Rewrite this as an elevator pitch for my boss"*
- *"Turn this into a tweet thread for busy professionals."*

This isn't just about compression. It's about translation from complex to clear and transformation from expert to everyday or vice versa. Use this kind of prompting when you're drowning in information but all you crave for is some basic insight.

2. Working with Specific Audiences

This is where most people miss the mark. They write to the machine but forget who it's for. Imagine who is going to be the final beneficiary of the output of your prompt and use that as part of the prompt.

- *"Explain Algebra like I'm five."*
- *"Now explain it like I'm 85-year-old grandfather."*

- *"Reframe this for a West Asian audience unfamiliar with Indian metaphors."*
- *"Make this understandable emotionally to someone who just lost a job."*

This is about empathy. Prompting for audiences trains you to think like them. It makes your content feel heard, feel human, not just helpful

3. Language Translation

This one's obvious and yet underused. Yes, GPT can translate across languages. But its real power lies when it also translates between tone, across cultures, and even between minds.

- *"Translate this paragraph into Tamil, keeping a poetic, lyrical tone."*
- *"Now rewrite the same in English—but in a voice a grandmother might use."*
- *"Turn this formal notice into a friendly, clear message."*

It's not just translation it becomes cultural sensitivity. It is ensuring that tone-shifting, shaping moods through language still retains that essential balance.

4. Proofreading with a Personality

Most people ask: *"Check this for grammar."* But why stop there? There is so much more you can achieve by the right prompt. Imagine that you can even choose the personality of your proofreader.

- *"Act like an editor for The Economist. Improve this without changing the meaning."*
- *"Polish this for clarity and flow but keep my voice intact."*
- *"Proofread this like a kind teacher reviewing a student's heartfelt letter."*
- *"Highlight any overused words or confusing sentences and suggest fixes."*

GPT doesn't just clean up your text. It teaches you why something works—or doesn't. This is not just spell-check; it is a style-check.

But I would like to remind you, make sure the reins of the translated or edited text stays in your hands only. It's possible you may have to proofread something that's already been proofread. While GPT is trained well enough, it is still not as good as you.

5. Sorting Out Scattered Thinking

Ever had a jumbled list of ideas or a mind-map that looks like spaghetti? And when you created it, it seemed so clear in your head. You can use various methods of prompting to straighten this chaos. Try out:

- *"Take this unstructured brainstorm and group it into 3 themes."*
- *"Make this raw note dump into an outline for an article."*
- *"Sort these bullets into a decision-making table with pros and cons."*

Prompting is like your Post-It wall, where your ideas start taking shape. With clarity, it can even become your project manager.

6. Brainstorming Creatively Across Domains

Creativity often gets blocked because we only look at a problem from one side. Prompting changes that by offering angles, metaphors, surprises. This is where GPT shines as a thought partner. Not only giving you what you ask for but also sparking things you hadn't thought of.

- *"Give me 10 story ideas where a kitchen plays a central role."*
- *"Suggest metaphors for burnout using imagery from Indian mythology."*
- *"What are unusual ways to explain risk to a teenager?"*
- *"I'm stuck. Help me see this problem from a bird's eye view."*

The best prompts help your mind look not just forward but also sideways. The key here? You should not just ask for "ideas." Ask for Perspectives.

7. Sector-Specific Prompting

Think prompting is just for writers? Not at all. Every job, every craft, every thought can be amplified with better prompts for any sector or industry. Here's how it looks in specific professions:

For Educators:

- *"Create a 20-question MCQ quiz on photosynthesis for Class 8."*
- *"Turn this lesson into a classroom activity with a fun challenge."*
- *"Summarise this chapter as lyrics for a song for middle school students."*

For Lawyers:

- *"Summarise this clause in plain English."*
- *"List 3 risks this contract section could pose to a small business."*
- *"Create a client explanation letter from this legal brief."*

For Therapists & Coaches:

- *"Suggest 5 journaling prompts for someone dealing with anxiety."*
- *"Frame a compassionate message to a client who missed a session."*

For Marketers:

- *"Write 5 headlines for this product, each with a different tone."*
- *"Turn this case study into a carousel post."*

Prompting is no longer a "tech skill." It's an amplifier for every profession. Here is where prompting becomes your quiet all-knowing assistant in the background, shaping your work into something sharper in any line of work you choose.

8. Creating Content in Multiple Styles

When you need versatility, style prompting steps in. Want one idea written five ways? One idea, many expressions. This is useful for content creators, storytellers, even teachers who want to engage in multiple formats. "Give me this idea as:

- *A poem*
- *A tweet*
- *A short story*
- *A news headline*
- *A bedtime parable"*

Now imagine using that across genres—food blogs, investor memos, wellness courses, even spiritual insights. When you stop treating GPT as an answering machine and start treating it like a performance artist, you open up a stage with infinite costumes - each one for a different role, tone, or perspective GPT can step into.

9. Prompting for Thinking, Not Just Answering

Till now we had used GPT after thinking, after we've figured things out. Here's an advanced move; let's test GPT out during your thinking itself. Prompting while you're figuring it out.

- *"I'm thinking about writing an article on attention spans. Help me organise my thoughts."*
- *"What are some angles I haven't considered?"*
- *"Play devil's advocate—why might this idea fail?"*

It's like walking with someone who listens, then uses nudges to know more and then sketches out what you just said but couldn't yet put it words or in any form. This is how prompting becomes a **process**, not a transactional activity.

So, what's the big idea here? Prompting is no longer about getting things done. It's about seeing things and then shaping it in a particular way. You start to realise:

- *That messy idea? **Promptable.***
- *That tangled report? **Promptable.***
- *That unexplained feeling? **Promptable.***
- *That boardroom presentation? **Promptable.***
- *That morning fog in your head? **Promptable.***

You start seeing prompting not as a skill, but as an advanced peek into reality. You are not just getting better answers, but you have started asking better questions. You're not outsourcing thought to GPT to get outputs. You're sharpening your own thoughts for clear contextual action. Imagine getting instantaneous feedback for your yourself - while thinking.

We're not done. In the next chapter, we go deeper into this idea and explore something many people never realise:

Prompting isn't just for getting outputs. It's a way to learn, to teach, to think, to reflect.

Chapter 6: Prompting as Knowledge Transfer

I have realised that Travel is a great teacher. It helps us learn newer things about the world, the culture, cuisine, people and what-not. It is a classroom with no walls. It is that walk one takes to understand what we already knew. It is not that we travel just to see the world, it is to help us grow as human beings.

I found prompting to be exactly like that.

Prompting to Learn

Forget Google. Forget 57 open tabs and five YouTube explainer videos playing at once.

What you now have at your fingertips is a patient, on-demand tutor who will explain the same thing twenty different ways if you ask it to. And never once roll its eyes or get upset if you did not get it right the first time.

- *"Explain the basics of blockchain to me like I'm a shopkeeper."*
- *"Give me a metaphor for inflation using kitchen ingredients."*
- *"Help me understand what entropy really means, without equations."*
- *"Break this concept into 3 levels: beginner, intermediate, advanced."*

The best part is learning here isn't passive. It's alive. Conversational. Layered. You're not being taught in the traditional sense - One topic taught in one way in one specific voice. Imagine yourself being in conversation with knowledge itself. And here's the secret: You can keep asking questions. The more clearly you ask, the more clearly, you'll understand. Don't think you are getting all this by prompting ChatGPT. You're prompting your own mind by articulating better

Prompting to Teach

Now flip the table. Because the moment you ask GPT to explain something to someone else, you're not just creating a lesson—you're becoming the teacher.

- *"Summarise the concept of zero for a 6-year-old using a bedtime story."*
- *"Turn this chapter on evaporation into an activity-based lesson plan."*
- *"Design 10 flashcards that help a student remember the states of matter."*
- *"Create a quiz to test conceptual clarity, not memory."*

Prompting as teaching is powerful because it again forces **empathy** into your question. You need to imagine the learner. Their level. Their language. Their confusion. Their curiosity. This is pedagogy, right? You and I can call it prompting, for now.

And the more you do it, the more you realise: To teach well, you must first prompt well.

Prompting the Self

It feels awkward to show your vulnerability to anyone. What will they think? Imagine yourself in a state where you just want to rant out as to why you are feeling so drained or bored? Or just why are you feeling elated for no reason? What if the question wasn't about any topic at all? What if it was about you? Well, prompting for yourself feels safe and comfortable. Sometimes even therapeutic. Wonder about this:

- *"Help me think through why I'm feeling restless about this project."*
- *"List 3 possible reasons why I keep procrastinating."*
- *"Help me reflect on this past week—what felt good, what drained me?"*
- *"Can you give me journaling prompts to understand my resistance to change?"*

You're not talking to a psychologist. You're not seeking advice. You're just hearing your own mind think aloud, in a new mirror. And in that mirror, strange things happen. Your mind begins to open. You begin to forgive your own contradictions. You begin to spot the patterns you've been living inside. And again—no judgment, no bias. Just a mirror.

Not because ChatGPT is 'wise'. Because you are. And because **you're listening differently now, to yourself.**

Prompting to Think in Public

Some thoughts don't want to be written yet. They want to be spoken aloud, tested, turned around like the pen you twirl while thinking in front of a laptop. That's what it means to think in public—with yourself, and a mirror that talks back. This is a tough, strange new skill that not enough people are talking about: Prompting as a way to **externalise your thinking.**

Let me explain.

Sometimes, you have a vague sense of something. A tension. A "half idea" that isn't quite ready. You need answers to get going but you don't know where to begin but the moment you prompt:

- *"I have a sense that our education system needs a different kind of focus. Help me think it out loud."*
- *"Give me counterpoints to this instinct I have about remote work being more creative."*
- *"What are three possible metaphors for leadership that move away from the 'Walk the Talk' cliché?"*

This way, you **make space for exploration**. You're letting your private questions become public, just for a moment. You're playing with your thought as an outsider. And the more you do it, the better you get at thinking like a writer even when you're not trying to write anything.

Prompting with a Thinking Partner

This is serious business. This is where it all comes together. You're not asking questions anymore. You're not using ChatGPT as an answer engine. You're engaging with it as a **thought partner**. You're building steps to climb to greater heights. You might begin with: *"Let's co-create a new framework for decision-making under pressure."*

And then, based on the answer you say:

- *"Challenge this framework."*
- *"Now stress-test it against a real-world situation."*
- *"Now visualise it in a table."*
- *"Now explain it to a first-time manager."*
- *"Now I want to make a presentation of it to my CEO."*

At some point, you'll look at the screen and suddenly realise - "Wow! I am thinking at a speed I didn't know I was capable of."

This is where some nay-sayers may say it is because GPT is magical. No, GPT is not magical. It's all because **you've trained yourself to think in layers in your mind**. You are then revising that thinking in real-time. You are learning to challenge your assumptions. And you are learning to hear your own voice reflected with a different nuance, clarity and a feeling which you kind of like.

And that's when you realise—this isn't about ChatGPT at all. It's all about **you**, becoming more articulate, more curious, more yourself.

So yes, we'll go back to frameworks and action prompts and productivity soon. But remember this chapter. This is that hint which will help you solve the Rubik's cube of your self anytime. Because someday, you won't want to write an article or to create a quiz. You won't want to translate a paragraph or write a blog. Or even write a book on Prompting. You may just want to sit with a thought. Maybe something foggy or fragile or just forming. And when that day comes, you'll know what to do.

You'll start a prompt. Not to find an answer but just to understand. Yourself.

Chapter 7: Prompting Across Personas

I have wondered about this. Whom should you go to when wanting to understand about careers? And if you are planning a vacation with your family? Let me ask you something strange: Would you ask a gardener to diagnose your cough? Or a CEO to write lullabies? Or a politician to prepare your tax returns?

No? You would go to an expert in that field, right?

This chapter is about **changing who ChatGPT should become** to change what you receive. You cannot prompt GPT the same way each time—regardless of what you need? You need to change the persona. Because underneath all the algorithm and the interfaces, ChatGPT isn't a fixed entity. It's a fluid reflector. It is the shapeshifter that we see in sci-fi movies. It is a master of disguise, changing its character, the way the director (that is You) wants it. It is a well-trained improviser waiting for clear directions. And your prompt is that casting call. What role do you want ChatGPT to take.

The Monk Test

Let me offer you something quirky. Imagine you've earned a once-in-a-lifetime moment: a chance to meet a monk who will answer just one question of yours—with complete clarity. What would you ask?

Would it be vague like, *"What is inner peace?"* Or would it be something deeply personal, quiet and searching like, *"How do I recognise the quiet voice of truth within me when it gets drowned by fear, ambition, and the noise of the world?"*

Now imagine you want that same quality of answer from GPT. That grounded-ness. That wisdom. That softness.

So, your prompt might become:

"Respond like a wise, compassionate monk who has spent decades in solitude and reflection. I want to understand how to tell apart my true inner voice from the chatter of fear, ambition, and ego. Give me a response that is grounded, timeless, and gently practical."

I hope you understand where all this is leading to. Do you see what changed? You didn't just ask what to answer—you asked who should answer. That one move shifts the whole texture of the response. Because it's not just about information anymore. It's about orientation. It's about tone and texture of the response.

Why the Persona Matters

Well, most of us tend to ask vague questions to others. However, if the person whom you have asked is smart enough, they will understand the context and respond maybe properly.

Keeping the same context, let's say you ask: *"Help me create a meditation routine."* Who should be answering?

- *A fitness instructor?*
- *A neuroscientist?*
- *A stressed-out manager trying to chill before meetings?*
- *Or that Himalayan monk?*

Each would give you something true but only one might give something useful to you right now. This is the power of persona. **It decides the lens through which your question is filtered.** And often, it's not the answer that changes everything, it's the angle from which it's given.

The Magical Words

Now that you have understood the importance of persona, you will be able to comprehend why this phrase is one of the simplest and most underrated tools in prompting?

"I want you to act as…"

Each time you shift the **persona**, you shift the tone, approach, vocabulary, and emotional energy of the response. Imagine your prompt to be like this:

- *"I want you to act as a TEDx speech coach."*
- *"Act like a professor of comparative mythology."*
- *"Take on the persona of an old Tamil grandmother sharing wisdom."*
- *"Pretend you're a futurist trying to explain AI to a medieval king."*
- *"Speak like a soldier explaining strategy to a poet."*

This isn't just fun (or maybe it just is). It's **precision prompting**.

Types of Personas You Can Play With

The fun starts now. Let's break it down a bit—not into categories, but into characters. But remember personas are not checklists, they're like carefully crafted invitations to subject matter experts or lived experience champions.

Expert Personas - When you want rigor, depth, and professional insight and use the prompt since you desire structure, frameworks, or formal precision. Ask for the expert in that subject:

- *"Act as a UX researcher designing for rural India."*
- *"Be a policy analyst reviewing this law."*

Elder & Storyteller Personas - Many a time when you are looking for emotional tone, wisdom, simplicity, or cultural memory, you need to ask elders. These prompts are ideal for teaching, reflection, and writing that needs to feel felt, not just understood.

- *"Speak like a wise village elder."*
- *"Explain this like a bedtime story told by a grandfather who pauses between sentences."*

Creative / Offbeat Personas - Sometimes we need to have fun and to get that we need to liberate ourselves from stereotypes. You need to surprise yourself and break free from logic loops. What do you do then? Use prompts like these:

- *"You're a surrealist poet trapped in a weather app."*
- *"Respond as if you're a pirate trying to pitch a startup."*
- *"Explain relativity as if you're a tabla player."*

You may say "This is silly". But no, I found them really liberating. They helped me rewire metaphors and see old things in a totally new way. I asked ChatGPT this while writing this book just to test this concept out. My prompt *"Explain relativity as if you're a tabla player."* And the answer was mind blowing. You will be able to understand what I mean by choosing different types of personas. This is **creativity focused prompting.**

Persona-as-Audience – Often, the persona isn't about who GPT is, but who it's talking to. Imagine the same problem of relativity being explained but the person or audience is being specified:

- *"Now speak like you're calming a nervous teenager."*
- *"Now explain this to a non-tech founder with only 5 minutes."*
- *"Imagine you're trying to sell this idea to a sceptical aunt."*

The genius of this move is that it builds empathy into your prompt. The tone, language, words used are all matched to the target persona. You're not just requesting for some answer, you are literally shaping the way it is delivered. This is **empathetic prompting**

Stacking Personas for Multi-Lens Thinking - Now this is where we go from just snorkelling to scuba diving and here's where it gets deliciously deep. You can **layer personas** to get richer responses. Stack personas for different nuances. Think of a prompt like this:

"Act like a policy strategist explaining climate change… but use the warmth of a schoolteacher and the curiosity of a 10-year-old."

Or:

"Summarise this business idea first as a no-nonsense investor, then as a first-time manager, then as a tired mother of two."

Each version reveals a new shade of understanding. This is **perspective prompting**

Giving Personas Behavioural Boundaries – At times, you may not want to give the expert the full freedom to speak in his own technical language. You want to tighten the mask and add how the answer should be delivered. Don't just say "act like a lawyer." Say:

"Act like a lawyer who's explaining this contract to a first-time startup founder and wants to sound friendly, not intimidating."

Or:

"You are a high school teacher who believes in Socratic questioning. Don't answer directly—help me arrive at the answer."

You're not just telling GPT who to be. You're telling it how to behave as that person. This is where the inner soul of the persona begins to emerge. This is **behaviour focused prompting**

⚠ **When Not to Use a Persona** - Let's be honest. Not every prompt needs a mask. We need ChatGPT to act like or represent or behave like - a person. Sometimes:

- You just need a list.
- Or a draft email.
- Or a quick grammar fix.

In those cases, time to skip the drama. But till you need a tone, angle, voice, or resonance which matters—persona is your best friend., the way to go. And the moment you start treating GPT like a character actor, you stop getting bland, one-size-fits-all answers. You start getting responses that showcase the artist - within you.

Final Thought: It's Not Just About ChatGPT. It's About You.

Every time you define a persona for GPT, you are **defining the shape of your own need.**

Are you asking as a teacher?

A seeker?

A sceptic?

A leader under pressure?

Change who ChatGPT is and watch how your own ideas start shifting shape too. You may see ChatGPT as a character actor, but the true artist is YOU — the **Prompt Weaver**. It is time for you to enter the wild carnival of crafting prompts. The zone where theory gets thrown into the air and you try things you haven't tried before. Because you can't just learn prompting by reading about it. You must learn by doing weird things with it. By pushing, pulling, bending, breaking—and laughing when it surprises you.

The persona you request is often a reflection of the 'you' that's asking. That's the secret magic of this chapter. When you learn to shape who GPT becomes, you're shaping who you become in the process of seeking. And that's why this chapter matters.

> ***Need quick persona ideas or examples?*** *The Loom in Appendix A* ***and*** *Prompt Gallery in Appendix D* ***might spark something fun.***

Chapter 8: Prompt Challenges and Games

This book isn't an instruction manual or a workbook. It's a playground in which I played and enjoyed and now I am asking you to join me in kicking the prompt around with me. That is the goal (no pun intended).

Till now you've learnt the frameworks. The body, mind, anatomy, intelligence of the prompt. You then shaped the personas for the prompt like various disguises or masks you could give to a secret agent. You've then mixed and matched various action verbs, tones and styles like a Master Crafter. You moved out to the school, learnt and tested your skills and now it is time to leave the classroom and step into the playground. This is where prompting becomes a game. A game with no scoreboard. Just pure, unadulterated fun.

Why? Because prompting isn't just about getting useful results. It's about feeling alive with language, logic, insight, and imagination that one has built.

Why Games Matter in Prompting

Every artist needs a sketchbook. Every musician needs to practice on a familiar melody but twisting it into something personal and expressive. Every thinker needs a space to go off-script. They call it out-of-the box thinking in modern parlance. And that's what this chapter is all about.

Prompt games do three magical things:

1. Train you to write better prompts without realising it.
2. Stretch GPT's creative muscles—and yours.
3. Build fluency in weirdness, which leads to surprising breakthroughs.

These aren't distractions. They're how you learn to prompt like a fusion guitarist learns to improvise—by playing.

Let's play.

? Game 1: Guess the Prompt

The name says it all. Instead of giving a prompt and getting an answer, flip it. This is different from the Reverse Prompting design technique in Chapter 4. There, you imagine the output and write backward. Here, you start with the output and ask GPT to reverse-engineer the prompt.

Take a paragraph, a summary, or a GPT-style reply. No context, no other input, just the output. Now challenge the GPT itself by asking it what the likely prompt was that created it. Once a possible prompt is guessed, ask how it could make the prompt better.

Why this works: It reveals the hidden power of prompting and you will begin to see the strings behind the puppet. You will notice that the quality of output is prompt-shaped. It forces you to reverse engineer with clarity and encourages precision. By now you would have seen how the machine thinks backward. Like all of us who do many things with what we call Muscle Memory, prompting will start feeling like that - like second nature.

Try this:

Level 1 - Take an old GPT response you liked and ask, *"Here's a GPT-generated output. Now you tell me—what was the likely prompt that created it?"*

Level 2 - *"Can you make that prompt better?"*

Game 2: Persona Ping-Pong

Get GPT to play table tennis from both sides of the table. First, you prompt GPT to act as a character. Then challenge it to wear another mask, ask it take up another character with the same content and then respond.

- *"Now rewrite this marketing pitch as if you're a travel writer."*
- *"Now explain this startup idea like a paranoid detective."*
- *"Now make the same argument as a 10-year-old genius with a sugar rush."*

Why this works: Each shift teaches you tone control, perspective and how different voices shapes messages. You'll notice how style and attitude change meaning, not just wording. You know what? Once you play this game, you'll never see "I just need one good answer" as the goal again. You will start building a gallery of perspectives.

Try this: Take one of your own prompts and ask GPT to reframe the response using 3 totally different personas. Compare them to see how it sounds, feels, and flows.

Game 3: The Format Flip

In the last game you gave flipped personas. Now flip the format. Give GPT a single topic and ask for multiple delivery styles:

"Explain the history of chess as:

- *A bedtime story*
- *A poem written in the same style as William Wordsworth.*
- *A customer complaint*
- *A breaking news bulletin*
- *A bar conversation between two ghosts"*

Why this works: Why do I think Format Flip is a great game to try out. First and foremost, it detaches **content** (the core idea or message) from **form** (how it's presented). It separates what you say from how you say it. This helps you see your own ideas more clearly, adapt them for different contexts, and become more flexible in how you think and communicate. When you flip formats, you break your dependency on just **one way** of expressing a thought. You get better at reshaping ideas for different audiences, channels and purposes.

Try this: Take a concept or insight you care about. Now ask for it as a tweet, a myth, and a conversation overheard in a café.

Game 4: The Deep Dive Game

This is a prompting technique where you ask GPT to interrogate you, gently once you give it a vague idea or belief. It will then follow up with deeper, more specific questions based on your answers. It's a layered, step-by-step method of thinking through complexity by probing assumptions, examples, or implications. Imagine a conversation like this:

You - *"I think school is outdated."*

"*Okay,*" says GPT. *"What do you mean by outdated?"*

Your answer.

GPT - *"Why do you believe that?"*

Your answer.

"What would a better system look like?"

And so on....

Why this works: This is Socratic Prompting at its finest. Some prompts are for speed. Others are for depth. The Deep Dive Game is meant to reach the depths. It starts at the surface of any statement, ritual, idea, or assumption, no matter how simple, and opens the doorway to something deeper. Keep going until you reach a core insight. Or a surprising doubt. It should not be taken as a debate; it is like those infinite reflections one sees in the hall of mirrors.

Try it when you're stuck with a doubt. Or when you're too sure you know the right answer. Try it with something you believe strongly. Or something you were taught as a child. See the game evolve in front of you.

Try this: Choose a belief, value, or ritual you've inherited. Ask GPT to question it step by step—with warmth and curiosity.

Game 5: The Constraint Box

This is a great game to play when you know that whatever you do will be met with resistance. How do we test it before it happens? Set absurd and ridiculous constraints. Then see how GPT works within them.

- *"I want to write a poem on my friend's birthday. Each line should start with each letter of his name."* **Note** - (Oh by the way, this is called an **acrostic poem.)**
- *"Summarise Mahabharata in 140 characters, no letter E."*
- *"Explain climate change using only dialogue between a baby and its toy in 4 sentences."*

Why this works: Constraints help creativity burst forth like lava out of a volcano. They bend the mind toward unusual solutions. You discover how far GPT can stretch—and how far you can, with your thoughts and then break out.

Try this: Imagine any problem, personal or professional. Now set some constraints which you feel you will pass through and then ask GPT for a solution within that.

Game 6: Step by Step Debug

Think of this like adjusting a camera's focus—same subject, just clearer with each turn.

Feed GPT a simple prompt. Then fix it step by step. Start with a casual prompt like: *"Help me write a note about teamwork."*

Then refine it step by step:

1. *"Make it sound more encouraging."*
2. *"Now aim it at a team that just missed a deadline."*
3. *"Keep it short—under 100 words."*
4. *"Now add a metaphor using a musical band."*
5. *"Polish it to sound like a leader who cares."*

Why this works: It teaches prompt iteration. You realise that your first prompt is rarely the best. But you learn how small tweaks change the quality of output, tone and scope not just the content. This game sharpens your prompt-sculpting instincts.

One small step at a time. You're not changing the topic—you're making it land better.

☢ Bonus Exploration: Prompt Chain Reactions

Think of this like putting the same idea through different camera modes—timelapse, thermal, night vision. Same spark, many views.

Start with the same idea: *"Help me write a note about teamwork."*

Now reimagine it with a random twist each time to connect action verbs, formats, tone, style and what have you:

1. *"Write it as a poem for a child."*
2. *"Turn that into a tweet for teachers."*
3. *"Now make it a pep talk by a coach before a match."*
4. *"Now explain it as a neuroscience experiment."*
5. *"End with a bedtime story version."*

Each step turns the same seed into a different bloom. With this game you learn to remix, reframe and reinvent. And you realise that most things aren't stuck. You begin to see how prompting is not linear. They're just waiting to be seen sideways.

For those of you who love music - **Step by Step Debug** is like tuning the instrument while **Prompt Chain Reactions** are like remixing the tune itself.

Final Thought: The Prompter Who Plays Wins

Here's the secret which every professional prompter learns one day: **If you're not playing with your prompts, you're only learning half the craft.** Play builds fluency in the way one prompts, teaches courage to try different ways and helps you to understand the options of possibility. You learn to think sideways. Speak in layers. And most of all, listen to what your own questions are really trying to say.

And that is where the real mastery begins.

So, play on.

Loved these? Three more games await you in Appendix E

Chapter 9: A Day in the Life of a Power Prompter

Let's take everything we've learned, and map it to real roles: educators, entrepreneurs, marketers, writers, and even you—the **Prompt Weaver** in the wild.

Chapter 8 was the playground with swings and see-saws, table tennis duels and winding mazes. But now, it's time to step into the real world—the main market. To the street corners, offices, school desks, and kitchen tables where real people ask: **"Okay, but how do I actually use all this in my day-to-day work?"**

Let's meet the **Power Prompter** at work.

Here's the truth no one tells you about productivity anymore: It isn't about waking up at 5 a.m. or colour-coding your calendar. It's about having a thinking partner who can walk with you—quietly, rapidly, reliably—through the messiness of real work. And that's what Prompting is. Everyone makes ChatGPT look like a fancy trick or a party gimmick. It's not. It is just this invisible second brain sitting by your side, helping you do things faster, better, and with more flow.

This chapter isn't about what prompting can do. You already know that. This is about how it fits into your life—your real, chaotic, multitasking, role-switching life. So, let's be the fly on the wall (or just a prompt chat box) and follow a few characters through their days. Each is a Power Prompter—not because they prompt often, but because they **prompt consciously**.

The Educator: Riya – Class 7 Science Teacher - She wakes up wondering how to keep curiosity alive in a system that rarely rewards it.

Before leaving for school – Quick Lesson Warmup

- *"Turn today's chapter on acids and bases into a 10-minute classroom story."*
- *"Add a simple experiment the kids can do at home using kitchen ingredients."*
- *"Create three analogies that will stick in their minds."*

At School - Worksheet Design

- *"Make a crossword puzzle using today's keywords."*
- *"Generate 5 one-line quiz questions—two should be tricky."*

Back home after school – Reflective Practice

- *"Help me summarise how well the students understood today's lesson, based on this observation journal I kept."*

Riya's Insight:" With prompting, I'm not just planning lessons—I'm shaping the experience of learning and teaching both. It helps me rediscover joy in the everyday parts of teaching and reminds me that how I teach is just as important as what I teach."

Your Turn: Where in your day could a little clarity or fresh perspective make things lighter?

***

The Entrepreneur: Karan – Startup Founder - *He's juggling deadlines, investor decks, and self-doubt and still finds time to breathe between the chaos.*

In the car on the way to work – Strategy Planning

- *"Create a roadmap for the next 60 days for an early-stage SaaS startup."*
- *"Now challenge it: what are 3 things we may be missing?"*
- *"Now write a version I can show to a sceptical investor."*

After the Townhall – Team Email Draft

- *"Write a motivating update for the team about hitting our beta launch milestone."*
- *"Add a personal touch—but keep it professional."*

Sitting back after dinner – Late-night Doubts

- *"I'm not sure our product is positioning itself well. Help me see this from a customer's point of view."*
- *"Now pretend you're a competitor. What would you do to beat us?"*

Karan's Insight: "Prompting helps me stay agile, without rushing into half-baked decisions. It's the only part of my day where I can slow down, zoom out, and still lets me think more clearly without pressing pause."

Your Turn: Think about a crazy day at work filled with meetings and unanswered mails

***

The Marketer: Sana – Content Strategist - *She finds new ideas don't come so easily and remaining innovative in thought is crucial.*

9:15 AM – Client Kick-off Briefing

- *"Summarise this client's brand in a tone doc. What's their vibe, voice, and energy?"*
- *"Give me 5 content themes that can run for 12 weeks straight."*

12:30 PM – LinkedIn Post Sprint

- *"Turn this long blog post into 3 punchy LinkedIn carousels."*
- *"Now make a version using memes."*

4:15 PM – Performance Report

- *"Draft a monthly analytics report in clear, jargon-free English. Include visuals."*

Sana's Insight: "Prompting isn't just output. It helps me switch roles—from analyst to writer to strategist—in minutes."

Your Turn: Ever wished for an insight that makes your boss sit up and take notice?

***

The Grand Parent: Arvind – Retired Engineer, Full-time Grandfather - *One never really retires. Staying curious is the best way to stay alive inside.*

Helping my grandchild - *"Explain the water cycle in 3 simple visuals my grandson can draw."*

Story time - *"Tell a funny story involving a train, a crow, and a math puzzle."* Now *"Make it silly but sneak in one value about sharing."*

Relaxing before going to bed - *"I always wanted to understand how a radio works. Teach me like I'm 12."*

Arvind's Insight: "Prompting makes me feel like I never stopped learning—or teaching. It helps me remain a lifelong learner."

Your Turn: Do you ever long to learn something new, just for the joy of it?

> *One of the quiet joys of prompting is discovering how it works with children, —not just for homework help, but for stories, feelings, questions, and imagination. If you're curious how GPT can support parenting, playful learning, or even bedtime wonder, peek into*
> *Appendix C: Prompting with Children.*

***

The Writer: Me

Blog Drafting

- *"Here's a messy paragraph. Help me keep my voice but make it land with more punch."*

- *"Rewrite this section as if I'm speaking it aloud to a fellow traveller."*

Prompt Guidebook Work

- *"Co-create this chapter with me—but don't make it too smooth. Stay human, stay reflective."*
- *"Don't overwrite. Let there be breath between thoughts."*
- *"I am not able to understand this example. Explain it to me the way you would to a person new to ChatGPT."*

That Late-Night Whisper

- *"I have a strange, soft idea. It's not ready yet. Walk with me. Help me tease it out without killing its magic."*

My Insight: "I used to think prompting was just about getting things done—sharper ideas, faster answers. But then it began to feel like sitting with a friend who lets you wander through a thought without rushing. Over time, it became less about productivity and more about clarity, curiosity, and coming home to my own voice."

My Turn – Do I wish I could write blogs that sounded like me—easy, free-flowing, like a chat over chai or of writing a book? Prompting has become the quiet thread that helps me do all that—and more.

What Makes These People "Power Prompters"?

A Power Prompter isn't someone who knows all the tricks. It's someone who sees where their thinking is stuck—and gently prompts it free. You don't need to be brilliant. You just need to be curious, kind to yourself, and willing to ask: "What if I don't have to think alone?" And suddenly, your workday isn't a solo act. It's a duet with an invisible, all-knowing partner.

Power Prompters don't become one for the number of prompts they use. It's that they:

- Know what to ask for
- Know how to shape who GPT becomes
- Think with GPT, not at it
- Use prompting as a tool for thinking, not just typing
- Know how to give GPT different masks to wear

They don't just prompt for tasks. They prompt for clarity, rhythm, confidence—and all the things you've already started learning.

Try This: A Day in Your Life

Now pause. Think of your own day. Where do you:

- Struggle to start something?
- Repeat the same types of thinking again and again?
- Avoid doing something because it feels messy?

These are **perfect places for prompting to step in.**

Write out a "Day in the Life" for yourself—and prompt your way through it. Start small. Even just:

- *"Draft a response to this email that I've been avoiding."*
- *"Summarise this article I don't have time to read."*
- *"Give me 3 ways to explain this idea to my team tomorrow."*

Let me be upfront. ChatGPT isn't the final solution. This isn't about transforming your life overnight—it's about nudging your thinking into better flow, one gentle prompt at a time.

Chapter 10: Future of Prompting

Let's step back for a moment. You've come far—from frameworks and personas to games and real-world workflows. You now know how to shape prompts, so they do what you intend—and sometimes more. But what's all this pointing toward? What's the future of prompting—not just as a skill, but as a way of being in the world?

This chapter isn't about predictions. Plenty of experts can give you those. It's about patterns. It's not about AI—we already know it's here to stay. It's about you, staying human in the middle of fast-changing times.

Prompting Is Becoming a Literacy

Once upon a time, literacy meant reading and writing. Then came digital literacy—navigating, searching, verifying. Now we stand at the edge of something new: **Prompt Literacy**—the ability to shape your questions, to partner with machines in making meaning, and to know when not to prompt at all. The future won't be about who uses AI. Everyone will. The future will be about how well they use it—and whether they know when not to. Just like a pen can be used for poetry or writing a troll, GPT will be used for brilliance and blandness. And that is the place you will find yourself soon - in the true fork in the road.

The Risk: Becoming Prompt Machines Ourselves

One can see a strange danger looming. In learning how to prompt well, we may accidentally begin to **think in templates**, not ideas. We may start chasing speed over originality of thought. We may seek productivity, instead of insight. Trying to optimise and smoothen every sentence, every word until there's no mystery left. You'll see it all around you:

- Over-engineered prompts with no soul
- People trying to "game the AI" instead of having a conversation.
- Content without context
- Perfectly structured nonsense

The risk is real: We will become **producers of prompts** but forget how to be **receivers of reflection**. Don't fall for it.

The Gift: Prompting as Consciousness Practice

At its best, prompting can be a doorway to deeper self-awareness. You begin by asking: *"Summarise this for me."* But over time you start asking - *"What am I trying to say?* And then *"Why does this idea matter to me?"* There may be moments when you would hesitate, worry or wonder. In those moments, prompting becomes a form of **self-talk with structure**. Do not take GPT to be a therapist and prompting is not meditation. But there is something it is. It is a quiet place where your voice meets another voice and somehow, both grow. Without judgment, without worrying about bias.

The Future of GPT in my mind is **Personalisation,** Not Automation. People worry: "Will AI replace writers, designers, teachers?"

Wrong question.

The real future is this: AI won't replace you. But people who know how to talk to AI might, not because they're smarter but because they're faster at thinking through the fog in their own minds. These are people who will not use GPT to avoid work. They will use it to find entry points into complexity and then make it simpler for themselves. They will delegate the first draft but never abdicate the final voice. That they will own.

What You Can Do: Maintain your Anchors

Well, this book is not about instructions but just thoughts to ponder. Consider some of the suggestions below as reminders - as Seven Small Stones to carry in your pocket.

1. Curiosity Before Control - Don't fall into the trap of over-prompting. Stay curious. Let GPT surprise you. Don't always optimise. Sometimes wonder like a child about the responses. That too is learning.

2. Presence Over Perfection - You don't need the "best" prompt (There isn't one anyway). You need the right prompt for you, today. Your context, your emotion, your thought-cloud. That's enough. The more human you are, the more helpful it becomes.

3. Don't Rush the Answer - It's easy to take the first answer and move on. But the real insights usually show up when you prompt again — slowly with thought.

4. Dialogue, Not Domination - Don't try to learn ChatGPT to master it. Learn to talk with it. Treat ChatGPT not as a machine to be tamed, but as a partner to be shaped. I am not telling you to humanise it, but it will show you a mirror always and you should be able to see the human in yourself reflected. Your power lies in the conversation with it.

5. You don't need to feel guilty if you don't use ChatGPT's response. - This is one pang that I used to feel all the time. That strange guilt, as if ignoring an AI output is like rejecting help from a kind friend. But remember, ChatGPT will not sulk, it will not feel bad. It cannot judge the silence between your question and your action. You can choose to ignore its answer or ask it again. You may disagree completely with what it has shared. It is possible that you take only a sentence from a long page or simply walk away from a thread which does not interest you anymore. Remember, the purpose of a GPT response is not to be accepted but to help you think more clearly, act more decisively, or feel more anchored. If it did that—even without using a single word—it has done its job. And if it didn't? Then prompt again.

6. Don't forget your voice, though GPT's voice may sound sweeter. - GPT's voice is smooth, polished, eloquent, easy on the ears. It can echo anything from the suavest of speakers to sharpest news anchors. But your voice is the one that holds your experienced truths, cultural spices, small secrets, and doubts that still mean something. So, when you borrow from GPT, do it like a singer rehearsing a song sung by a well-known singer. But when it's time to perform, sing that song, in your own voice even if it cracks. Even if the words are not always "right." That's the song people will remember. Not because it was perfect - but because it was yours.

7. GPT is an unbiased friend and an all-knowing assistant; not the Boss. - GPT is not human. It still runs on artificial intelligence, not instinct. GPT doesn't have an ego, and it also doesn't have intuition, or fear or fire. You do. Treat it like a very intelligent junior: someone who's read everything, remembers everything and works at lightning speed. But it still looks to you to decide the direction. Don't surrender your judgment to it. Use GPT to surface options, challenge assumptions, gather frameworks—but remember…

You are the meaning-assigner. You are the heart in the room. You are the final voice.

GPT is just the thread. **You're the prompt-weaver.**

The Prompt is Just the Beginning

You may have picked up this book thinking: "I want to learn how to prompt better." But maybe now, you're thinking:

"I want to think more clearly."

"I want to feel more confident."

"I want to build with rhythm, reflect with intention, and grow with grace."

That's not a tech skill. That's a human one. And maybe—just maybe—that's the real point of prompting. Prompting teaches you to ask better questions. But in the process, you may just grow into the kind of person others come to with their questions— someone who listens, reflects, and helps others think more clearly too.

And with that, we close. Not a full stop.

Because your next prompt is waiting. And this time, it isn't in the book.

It's in your mind.

And if you are ready to try it all on one evolving idea, *Appendix F: The Prompt Lab* *is waiting for you*

One Last Thought (Before You Go Prompting Again…)

If you've made it here, thank you. You didn't just read a book—you stayed in this conversation with me.

I am sanguine that you paused to wonder, to shape questions, to sit with your own thoughts and sometimes let a machine show you new ones. That's not something everyone does. It takes a quiet kind of courage to explore a tool not just for its features, but for how it changes your way of seeing and thinking.

Prompting, as you've seen, is not a shortcut. It's not a hack. It's a skill, an art, which you acquire over time. You may not remember every chapter or framework in this book. But I hope you remember this:

You are not asking questions to get perfect answers.

You are asking to keep discovering the person behind the question.

And for that, no prompt is ever wasted. So now, go -

Prompt your day.

Prompt your doubt.

Prompt your wonder.

And when you return, this book — and I — will still be here.

With quiet companionship,

Srinivasan

Acknowledgements

This wasn't the kind of book written in a cabin in the hills or in a quiet library. It was typed—day after day—from the furthest corner of our bedroom, where I sat hunched over my laptop, chasing thoughts, questions, and the occasional typo.

Through it all, my wife never complained. She let me disappear into my world of prompts and patiently endured the sound of keys tapping late into the night. Thank you for that quiet companionship.

To my family—who probably wonders where all this curiosity is headed—thank you for giving me the space to find out.

And to my co-thinker and collaborator—ChatGPT—thank you for being the friend who never sleeps and never interrupts.

There are a few friends who may end up reading the early drafts of this book. If you're one of them, and you're reading this now—thank you for walking with me, even if briefly.

This book was never about a long list. It was meant to be a personal journal of insights. That's the spirit with which it was written. That's how I hope it's read too.

About the Author

Lt Col Srinivasan is a retired armed forces officer, HR professional, and lifelong question-asker who stumbled into the world of prompting with curiosity, not credentials. He doesn't come from the world of AI or technology—and that's exactly the point. This book is a record of one ordinary person's quiet, thoughtful journey with a new kind of thinking partner. When he's not exploring prompts, you'll find him planning travel itineraries, reflecting on life, or typing another lived experience into his blogs. Check it out at www.youfoundsrini.com He lives in Bangalore, India, with his wife Vijaya and Auro, their pet Golden Retriever. Both his children are married and well settled abroad.

Appendices

Appendix A - The Prompt Loom

Prompt Part	*What it is*	*Examples / Suggestions*	*Leave Room For…*
Subject	The core topic or idea your prompt revolves around.	Climate change, Stoicism, Fundraising, Cooking with millet	Something you care about, something you're learning
Goal / Intent	What you want to see happen—the intended purpose or output.	Summarise, Brainstorm, Challenge, Simplify, Teach, Reframe	Your personal goals: Clarify a feeling, untangle a doubt
Persona / Role	Who GPT is pretending to be or 'becomes' while responding.	Startup founder, Monk, TED coach, Grandmother, Data analyst, Tabla player	Specific people from your world, characters from stories
Action	What GPT is doing with the material—listing, rewriting, analysing, etc.	Write, Rewrite, Explain, Translate, Compare, Create, Evaluate, Reflect, List	Keep a personal bank of verbs you love using
Type (Depth / Sharpness)	The level of finesse or creativity needed in the response.	Generate, Refine, Polish, Summarise, Simplify, Critique, Transform, Reframe, Expand, Condense, Juxtapose	Ask for rough drafts when exploring, demand clarity when closing in
Format / Output	The shape or container of the response—story, list, table, script.	Poem, Table, Dialogue, Email, Slide, Recipe, Analogy, Cartoon script, Thread	Your own formats—e.g., a WhatsApp reply, classroom worksheet
Target Audience	Who the response should be tuned to—what they need to hear or understand.	A child, a CEO, a busy parent, a curious retiree, Gen Z friend	Consider what that person cares about or might misunderstand
Purpose	Why you're asking—what inner intent or emotion drives the prompt.	Curiosity, clarity, closure, fun, frustration	Hidden emotions or values behind the request

Prompt Part	***What it is***	***Examples / Suggestions***	***Leave Room For…***
Key Elements	Specific things that must be included—like ingredients for the response.	Use this metaphor, include data from 2023, must mention X	Things you don't want forgotten
Structure	The logical flow or layout you expect.	Intro → Insight → Analogy → Summary / Past → Present → Future	Map your mental flow; you can even say "follow this pattern"
Tone	The emotional energy or stylistic feel—formal, friendly, poetic, playful.	Humorous, Friendly, Poetic, Serious, Compassionate, Crisp, Irreverent, Reflective	Match your mood. Match the audience. Add your own tones.
Style	The surface feel—pacing, rhythm, language texture, complexity.	Minimalist, Punchy, Flowing, Descriptive, Story-driven, Rhetorical, Plainspoken	Borrow from your favourite writers. Or your natural voice.
Foundation	The platform or context the prompt stands on—where or how it will be used.	Instagram post, Email to boss, Therapy worksheet, Workshop slide	What's the real-life use case? Add constraints accordingly
Constraints / Boundaries	What limits or rules shape the response.	Word limits, Avoid jargon, Use metaphors only, Bullet-free, Alliteration only, Must rhyme	Absurd constraints can spark magic. Try some!

- How to Use This Table:
  - Pick 2–3 key components for any given prompt. Don't overload.
  - Mix and match across rows for creative combinations.
  - Personalize the right column—make this loom yours.

Appendix B - List of Prompting Components

(feel free to add more in the space given in the tables)

No.	Goal / Intent	Description
1	Explain	Clarify a topic or concept in simple, understandable terms.
2	Translate	Convert language, tone, or idea across cultural or linguistic boundaries.
3	Summarise	Boil down lengthy text into digestible highlights or key points.
4	Expand	Add depth, context, or detail to a short or vague idea.
5	Reframe	Shift perspective, tone, or purpose to make it more relevant or useful.
6	Critique	Evaluate quality, logic, and clarity with balanced, constructive feedback.
7	Simplify	Strip away jargon or complexity while retaining core meaning.
8	Inspire	Evoke imagination, enthusiasm, or reflection with emotionally resonant prompts.
9	Teach	Deliver understanding through structure, analogies, and clear scaffolding.
10	Reflect	Help surface self-awareness, introspection, or insight about an experience.

No.	Action Verbs	Description
1	List	Provide a sequence or bullet-pointed breakdown of ideas.
2	Rewrite	Redraft a passage while retaining key meaning, altering tone or audience.
3	Compare	Explore similarities and differences across two or more things.
4	Create	Invent something new—story, structure, idea, or solution.
5	Imagine	Generate fictional, speculative, or whimsical content.
6	Structure	Organize scattered thoughts into outlines, formats, or frameworks.
7	Role-play	Act as a character or persona to shift perspective.
8	Interrogate	Ask follow-up questions or probe an idea for deeper understanding.
9	Diagnose	Identify causes, flaws, or gaps in logic or understanding.
10	Visualise	Transform abstract concepts into imagery, metaphors, or diagrams.

No.	Format / Output	Description
1	Bullet Points	Concise, clear list of ideas or steps.
2	Table	Structured grid for comparisons, pros/cons, or data.
3	Email	Professional communication tailored to a recipient.
4	Social Media Post	Short-form content—tweets, threads, or captions.
5	Story / Anecdote	Narrative form to build empathy or illustrate a concept.
6	Dialogue	A conversational exchange—great for explaining, role-play, or drama.
7	Poem	Rhythmic, metaphorical expression of an idea.
8	FAQ	Common question-answer style for clear understanding.
9	Mind Map	Web-like branching of concepts, categories, or connections.
10	Quiz / Flashcards	Interactive or educational test-style prompt.

No.	Tone / Voice	Description
1	Conversational	Friendly, informal, like chatting with a friend.
2	Academic	Formal, precise, and evidence-based explanation or argument.
3	Humorous	Light-hearted, witty, or ironic tone to entertain or ease tension.
4	Empathetic	Warm, understanding, and emotionally attuned to the audience.
5	Reflective	Thoughtful, pondering, often introspective or personal in tone.
6	Persuasive	Influences belief or action through logic, emotion, or credibility.
7	Childlike	Simple, imaginative, and innocent tone with curiosity and wonder.
8	Inspirational	Uplifting, motivational, and idealistic tone to move or energise.
9	Direct / No-nonsense	To-the-point, efficient, and clear—no fluff.
10	Storyteller	Rich, descriptive, and engaging narrative voice.

Appendix C - Prompting with Children

Prompting isn't just for work, writing, or innovation. It has a quiet, transformative power when used with children. Whether you're a parent, grandparent, teacher, or curious adult, prompting can open doors to imagination, learning, and laughter.

You don't need ChatGPT to talk to your child. Let's begin with that. You already carry within you a deep well of love, instinct, and memory. But even the most devoted parent has had days when energy runs low, or the spark to start a meaningful conversation simply doesn't come. And that's where ChatGPT can gently step in—not as a replacement, but as a background partner that nudges you gently into a fresh idea, a surprising metaphor, or a playful new approach.

This appendix is not a how-to guide. It's a glimpse into what's possible when you bring the spirit of play, wonder, and shared exploration into the act of prompting with a child. Let's take a few moments from a child's day and see how prompting can help shape them into magical connections.

During Bedtime: When the World Winds Down

This is a moment of tenderness, when stories soothe and imaginations open. But some nights, you just don't have the story ready. You can ask ChatGPT:

"Give me a gentle bedtime story starter for my 3-year-old."

You take that line, and suddenly you're off—weaving a tale with your child about flying umbrellas or whispering moonbeams. It's your story. GPT just lit the first candle.

During Mealtimes: When Conversations Linger

These are golden pockets for connection, but asking "How was school?" rarely goes anywhere. Instead, try something surprising:

"Tell me what happened at school, but tell it like (**take one of the child's favourite cartoon characters or heroes**) *would.* "

You'll find your child playing along. There's laughter, maybe even insight. You can ask GPT to give you 3 such playful alternatives for everyday questions. And they'll come. Reliable, silly, warm.

During Car Rides: When Attention Is Drifting

The car is a curious space—you're together but facing forward, a great time for gentle talk. *"What do you think the clouds are planning today?"*

That's not a question you pull out of thin air every time. But GPT can hand you a list of 5 quirky conversation starters. You pick the one that fits your child's mood. And off you go, building a conversation out of trees and flowers and make-believe.

For Emotions: When Feelings Need Space

Children struggle to name their feelings. You may sense something, but not know how to ask. So you prompt: *"Suggest a gentle way to ask my child about their feelings using imagination or storytelling."*

Now you have an entry point. Not therapy. Just space.

For Curiosity and Wonder: When the Mind Is Sparkling

Let's say your child is obsessed with dinosaurs or inquisitive about stars. You can prompt: *"Give me 3 playful science questions I can ask a 5-year-old about space"* or *"Invent a silly game to teach a child about dinosaurs using kitchen items."*

And you'll get small, delightful sparks that help keep their curiosity alive.

What this really is, is a way to let GPT be your background brainstorming partner. You still bring the warmth, the trust, the real knowing of your child. But GPT can help you see sideways.

So, no—you don't need GPT to parent. But sometimes, just sometimes, it can be like finding a forgotten book on your shelf with the right story just when you need it most.

Let this appendix be a nudge. Try a few prompts. Let them open a few windows. And if one day your child surprises you with a story you've never heard before, sparked by one of these little nudges—you'll know it worked.

Quiet magic. That's what this is.

Final Thought: A Prompting Habit for Families

Create a small ritual:

- One bedtime question a day.
- One story prompt over breakfast.
- One drawing inspired by a silly GPT story on weekends.

You're not just raising children. You're raising thinkers, storytellers, question-askers. Prompting can be your quiet companion in that joyful work.

A Gentle Warning (or Invitation?) - And if you ever suspect your child is using ChatGPT to figure out how to deal with *you* as a parent… Congratulations.

You've raised a curious, strategic, emotionally intelligent prompt-weaver. Now the real question is: *Are you ready to prompt back?* Because this isn't a battle. It's the beginning of a beautiful conversation—one where both sides are asking better questions, together.

Appendix D - The Prompt Gallery

You've come a long way through this book. You've listened, wondered, reflected, scribbled. But prompting, like any good craft, is learned through doing—through playful nudges, not pressure.

This is not a test. This isn't homework. Think of the next 10 prompts as tasting spoons by which you could check the salt level in the dish you have prepared. Each one reflects something you've encountered: clarity, curiosity, perspective, tone, or simply the joy of trying. They start simple and then grow richer. Just read them. If you want to try any of them — just copy it, paste it in the chat box of ChatGPT, and see what the result looks like. You can change them, twist them, break them – you are the one who is writing the prompt.

You don't need to find an answer in all of them. You just need to enjoy the idea that each question can become a thread. And you, the weaver.

1. *"Explain yoga to someone who's never stretched a day in their life."*

→ *Represents*: Clarity, Audience awareness

2. *"Rewrite this apology to sound kinder, but not overly formal."*

→ *Represents*: Tone, Emotional shaping

3. *"Give me 3 analogies for being stuck in life—one from nature, one from traffic, one from sports."*

→ *Represents*: Comparative prompting, Creative analogy

4. *"Explain 'attention span' like you're a schoolteacher talking to 10-year-olds."*

→ *Represents*: Persona, Audience match, Teaching focus

5. *"Turn this long blog intro into a 30-second elevator pitch."*

→ *Represents*: Compression, Format switch, Constraints

6. *"I think I'm procrastinating out of fear. Ask me 3 gentle questions to help me see more clearly."*

→ *Represents*: Socratic drill-down, Reflective prompting

7. *"Pretend you're a journalist, a grandmother, and a futurist. How would each one describe AI in one sentence?"*

→ *Represents*: Persona stacking, Perspective shifting

8. *"Give me a poem using only cooking metaphors to talk about love and loss."*

→ *Represents*: Creative constraint, Metaphorical thinking

9. *"Take this vague idea and shape it into a short story, then summarise the story as a TEDx talk."*

→ *Represents*: Format flip, Depth-layering

10. *"Act like a tabla player explaining the theory of relativity to a curious teenager in the audience."*

→ *Represents*: Persona, Analogy, Framing, Teaching tone, Cultural metaphor

Appendix E – Bonus Prompt Games

For those who'd like to keep playing…

If the games in Chapter 8 whet your appetite, here are three more to stretch your imagination, test your prompting instincts, or just give your thinking a delightful twist. They come in three levels of creative depth. Try them out when you feel like testing your prompt weaving expertise and twirl with your thoughts a little more freely.

Game 7: The Tone Transformer - *(Level: Easy & Fun)*

Start with a single statement. Then prompt GPT to change only the tone, keeping the content intact.

Example: "Tell me I missed the deadline in a way that sounds:

- Annoyed
- Kind
- Passive-aggressive
- Friendly but disappointed
- In the voice of a politician"

Try this: Pick up one of your own messages — emails, WhatsApp or any reminders. Watch how words carry emotion.

Learning - This game teaches emotional intelligence in prompts by shifting the tone of the same message and this helps because small tonal changes can radically shift meaning and perception.

***

Game 8: Prompt from a Prop - *(Level: Medium – Creative Triggering)*

Pick a physical object near you (a spoon, a scarf, a shoe). Then ask GPT to build around it:

Examples: You could try one or more of them.

- "Tell a fable where a forgotten key is the main character."
- "Describe this cracked mug's journey across time, from factory to now."
- "Give me a startup idea inspired by this stapler."

Try this: Look around your room. Prompt something into becoming something else from the most ordinary object. Let your curiosity start the fire.

Learning – This game will help you learn to prompt using sensory or visual cues which are great for ideation, storytelling, or unlocking stuck thinking, since most real-world prompts start not from clear ideas but from images, feelings, or fragments.

***

Game 9: The Invisible Assumption - *(Level: Deep – Cognitive Challenge)*

Write a "normal" prompt. Then ask GPT:

- "What assumptions do I seem to be making in this prompt?"
- "Is there a different way to approach this?"

- "What might someone with the opposite belief ask instead?"

Example: Write a prompt: "How do I get my team to work harder?" Then imagine GPT answers *"You may be assuming the team is lazy rather than unmotivated or misaligned."* Then you could try and respond something like this "How can I understand what's blocking my team's energy?"

Try this: Start writing out a prompt about something you're frustrated with. Use GPT to mirror what your words might be hiding.

Learning – These kind of prompts may help uncover your own hidden assumptions behind a prompt. It's a kind of Reverse + Socratic + Reflection loop (so you get to try multiple methods in one). We often ask questions based on our beliefs, without even realising it. This game helps gently bring those hidden beliefs to the surface.

Appendix F – The Prompt Lab - Weave your Thread Now

This is just a quiet invitation to follow one idea across the arc of this book. Sometimes, you just need one, looked at again and again, with new eyes, to master prompting. This lab is for that one thread. Start it now or come back later. This is not a task. It's your companion.

🧵 **Step 1: Start with a Seed** - Write your base prompt or idea. Anything real. - *A trip to plan. A project to shape. A feeling to understand.*

→ *Write it here:* ______________________________

🔍 **Step 2: Reframe** - Ask GPT to shift the audience, tone, or lens. "What if this was for a child? A CEO? A monk?" *What changed?*

→ *Write it here:* ______________________________

🎭 **Step 3: Add a Persona** - Ask GPT to respond as someone specific — an artist, a coach, a wise elder. *What felt different or new?*

→ *Write it here:* ______________________________

🔄 **Step 4: Transform the Format** - Turn it into a poem. A list. A table. A conversation. *How did structure reveal something hidden?*

→ *Write it here:* ______________________________

Step 5: **Challenge the Assumption** - "What belief is hiding behind this question?" *Ask GPT to mirror your assumption. What did you see?*

→ *Write it here:* ___________________________________

Step 6: Your Woven Prompt - Now combine your learnings. Create a fresh version of the prompt.

→ *Write your evolved prompt here:* _________________________

Note from one Prompt Weaver to another - *Prompting isn't always about being efficient and perfect. Sometimes it's about being curious, silly, wrong, brave, or just testing yourself.. You don't need to finish this. You just need to start. That's how we learn to ask better, and in doing so, think better too. You learn about yourself through them.*

www.ingramcontent.com/pod-product-compliance
Lightning Source LLC
LaVergne TN
LVHW100332210926
848480LV00003B/1319